T0197493

What Kind of Princess Are You?

WRITTEN BY SHERYL A. JONES

ILLUSTRATIONS BY KEN HOSKIN

Copyright © 2022 by Sheryl A. Jones. 835918

All rights reserved. No part of this book may be reproduced
or transmitted in any form or by any means, electronic
or mechanical, including photocopying, recording, or by
any information storage and retrieval system, without
permission in writing from the copyright owner.

This is a work of fiction. Names, characters, places and
incidents either are the product of the author's imagination
or are used fictitiously, and any resemblance to any actual
persons, living or dead, events, or locales is entirely
coincidental.

To order additional copies of this book, contact:
Xlibris
844-714-8691
www.Xlibris.com
Orders@Xlibris.com

ISBN: Softcover   978-1-6698-1440-5
       EBook   978-1-6698-1441-2

Print information available on the last page

Rev. date: 04/05/2022

What Kind of Princess Are You?

Written by Sheryl A Jones M.Ed.

Dedicated to my daughter Cassandra Ann Jones and all of the little girls I have taught in my 33 year teaching career.

We roll out the royal carpet to girls around the world. A beautiful princess can be found in every little girl!

You may be a princess that likes to jump rope in your bedroom.

You may be a princess that likes to look in the mirror and eat spaghetti with a spoon.

Three beautiful Princesses all in a row. The first one uses crutches to help her go where she must go.

The one in the middle has two devices to help her hear.

The last one wears glasses so she can see things clear.

These princesses have different crowns. Look at the beautiful colors and designs that are found!

They look different in a special way.

Their smiles can brighten up a sad day.

Princesses from many places with very pretty faces.

They are awesome, magnificent, powerful, and brave! All of this is true.

What kind of Princess are you?

Insert your picture here.

Printed in the United States
by Baker & Taylor Publisher Services